GRAYBEARD
★ LECTURES ★

The Lighter Side of the Dark Arts of Selling

from the Whiteboard of
Mark "Dr. Maddog" Donnelly, PhD.

RPSS PUBLISHING – BUFFALO, NEW YORK

drmaddog@hotmail.com

Graybeard Lectures - The Lighter Side of the Dark Arts of Selling

Perfect Bound ISBN: 978-1-956688-64-1

Printed in the United States of America

10 9 8 7 6 5 4 3 2 1

RPSS Publishing - Buffalo, New York

Welcome to my Whiteboard.

Today, we'll discuss
these clues I've learned as a
high mileage Graybeard –
buried in a flurry of bullet points.

Please excuse my handwriting.

TABLE OF CONTENTS

The Lighter Side of the Dark Arts of Selling
(With a Detour Through Freud's Living Room)

Every profession has a version it puts on the brochure and another it mutters about over coffee.

Selling is no different.

The brochure version is clean, logical, and filled with arrows pointing upward. It speaks confidently about value propositions, customer journeys, and best practices. It insists that decisions are made carefully, rationally, and in the correct order.

The coffee version knows the truth.

A Gentle Graybeard Admission

After enough years in the room, you start noticing something funny.

The decision usually happens before the explanation.

Often before the meeting.

Sometimes before anyone finishes sitting down.

You can see it when shoulders drop. When the room stops fidgeting. When questions quietly shift from why to how.

That's not enthusiasm.

That's relief.

The sale didn't happen.

It concluded.

Everything after that is choreography.

About That "Dark Art" Thing

Calling it a dark art makes it sound dramatic, possibly involving cloaks or chanting. It's nothing so theatrical.

The dark art of selling simply lives in places we don't like to acknowledge:

- Tone
- Timing
- Familiarity
- Silence
- The blessed absence of pressure

We call it dark not because it's sinister, but because it operates in the background, politely avoiding attention.

Like plumbing.

Or competence.

Why This Is the Lighter Side

This book is not here to teach manipulation, persuasion tricks, or psychological ambushes.

Those are the heavy side of the dark arts. They require effort, drama, and eventually apologies.

The lighter side is easier on everyone involved.

It's about understanding how people actually decide and then not getting in their way. About removing friction instead of adding urgency. About realizing that the most persuasive move is often to stop trying so hard.

It's selling with a relaxed grip.

The Myth We Maintain for Appearances

Publicly, we pretend selling is a rational exchange of i   nformation.

Privately, we know the human brain is more interested in feeling settled than being correct.

Logic doesn't lead.

It tidies up afterward.

This is not a flaw. It's an efficiency feature. If humans had to fully analyze every decision, we'd still be standing in grocery aisles comparing salt.

A Short Historical Detour *(Because This Isn't New)*

These dark arts didn't begin with marketing departments.

They began the moment one human tried to convince another human that this was the better cave, berry, or trade route.

Early selling was never about features. It was about reducing fear.

Later, markets added stories. Authority added symbols. Merchants learned that confidence traveled faster than truth and familiarity beat novelty almost every time.

Then, in the early 20th century, psychology officially entered the room and politely closed the door.

Edward Bernays, nephew of Sigmund Freud, applied psychoanalytic ideas to advertising and public relations and accidentally confirmed what sellers already knew but rarely admitted:

People don't buy products.
They buy relief, identity, belonging, and permission.

Selling didn't become manipulative at that moment.

It became honest, just without the courtesy of saying so out loud.

Why Graybeards Smile at Meetings

Graybeards have watched every new selling trend arrive breathless and leave quietly.

We've learned that volume is usually compensating for something missing earlier. That urgency often means insecurity. That the best salespeople sound less like performers and more like calm guides who know where the light switches are.

They don't argue about tactics anymore.

They watch behavior.

And they smile when the room decides before the slide deck loads.

What This Book Actually Does

This book shines a little daylight into the dark art.

Not to ruin it.

Just to demystify it.

You'll learn why:

- people say yes to end tension, not to gain features

- trust is built by consistency, not promises

- effort can be a warning sign

- quiet strategy outperforms noise in the long run

None of this requires tricks.

Just attention.

A Final Graybeard Note

Once you see this, you can't unsee it.

You'll start noticing decisions forming in rooms before anyone talks. You'll hear logic scrambling to catch up. You'll realize how often the sale you're trying to make is already done—and how often people ruin it by continuing to try.

You'll talk less.

Listen more.

Pause longer.

And you'll discover something surprisingly pleasant.

The lighter side of the dark art of selling is that when you stop trying to look persuasive, people decide on their own.

Which is, frankly, less work for everyone.

The quiet stuff does most of the heavy lifting.

Turn the page.

We'll start with the oldest trick of all: understanding which part of the brain is actually in charge.

How the Brain Actually Buys
(And Why We Pretend It Doesn't)

Before we go any further, we need to clear the room.

Not physically. Mentally.

Because Part I asks you to set aside one of the most comforting myths in business: that people buy because they are convinced by logic, persuaded by facts, or impressed by well-structured arguments.

> That myth is tidy.
>
> It fits on slides.
>
> It makes meetings feel productive.
>
> It is also wrong.

Graybeards learn this the slow way, by watching smart ideas fail and simple ones quietly succeed. You can have the better product, the better price, and the better pitch and still lose, not because the market is irrational, but because the human brain is doing exactly what it was designed to do.

The Brain Was Never Designed for Your Funnel

The human brain did not evolve to evaluate options, compare feature sets, or scroll pricing tables. It evolved to keep us alive with as little effort as possible.

> Speed mattered.
>
> Certainty mattered.
>
> Familiar patterns mattered.

Those instincts didn't disappear when commerce showed up. They just changed costumes.

Today, the threats are social, financial, and emotional instead of tooth-based, but the decision machinery is the same. The brain still asks, Is this safe? Does this feel right? Can I trust this?

Only after those questions are answered does it allow logic to speak.

Why We Keep Getting This Backwards

Selling culture talks about rationality because rationality flatters us.

It lets us believe we are objective, measured, and in control. It allows organizations to confuse preparation with progress and activity with understanding.

Emotion, instinct, and subconscious reaction feel inconvenient. They don't follow neat frameworks. They don't respect org charts.

So we ignore them.

And then we're surprised when the numbers don't move.

What Part I Will Do

Part I is not about techniques.

It's about anatomy.

We're going to look at:

- how decisions are actually made
- why the "rational customer" is a comforting fiction
- and why logic consistently arrives after the decision has already been made

This is not a call to abandon thinking. It's a call to respect order.

Emotion first.

Logic second.

Get that sequence wrong, and no tactic in the world will save you.

A Graybeard Warning Label

If you are looking for quick tricks, scripts, or psychological hacks, this is the wrong section of the book.

What follows may feel unsettling at first, especially if you've built a career on explaining things well. It suggests that clarity alone is not enough and that persuasion is often the wrong goal entirely.

That discomfort is useful.

Pay attention to it.

It's the sound of an old assumption loosening its grip.

Why This Matters Now

In a world saturated with messaging, attention has become selective and trust has become scarce.

People no longer give you the benefit of the doubt. They give you the benefit of pattern recognition.

Part I lays the groundwork for everything that follows by answering a simple but often ignored question:

Who is really in charge of the buying decision?

Once you understand that, selling gets quieter, simpler, and far more effective.

Turn the page.

The brain is already listening.

CHAPTER 1

Two Brains Walk Into a Store

(Only One of Them Buys)

Two brains walk into a store.

The first one doesn't say a word.

The second one immediately starts taking notes.

The quiet one looks around.

The note-taker asks where the bathrooms are and whether there's Wi-Fi.

If you've spent any time in selling, marketing, fundraising, or persuading a teenager to eat a vegetable, you already know which one is in charge.

Meet the Decider

The first brain is old. Very old.

It predates commerce, language, and brand strategy decks with inspirational stock photography. It was designed for survival, not quarterly earnings. Its job description is simple:

keep the organism safe and moving forward with minimal effort.

This brain makes decisions quickly because, historically speaking, hesitation was a bad idea.

> It doesn't analyze.
>
> It senses.
>
> It doesn't debate.
>
> It reacts.

It asks questions like:

- Does this feel safe?

- Is this familiar?

- Do I trust this?

- Can I get out of here if I need to?

If the answers are acceptable, it allows the interaction to continue. If not, it quietly reaches for the exit. No announcement. No appeal. Just a subtle internal "nope."

This is the brain that buys.

Meet the Explainer

The second brain shows up later, usually when someone asks, "So why did you choose this one?"

This brain loves reasons.

It enjoys comparisons.

It respects bullet points and spreadsheets.

Its job is not to decide.

Its job is to explain the decision in a way that sounds intelligent, defensible, and appropriate for professional company.

This is the brain that says things like:

- "The value proposition was stronger."

- "It aligned better with our strategic goals."

- "After careful consideration…"

None of that is untrue. It's just not the beginning of the story.

It's the press release.

The Order of Operations Problem

Most selling fails because it speaks to the explainer first and hopes the decider will catch up.

That's like sending a résumé to a smoke alarm.

The decider doesn't care how much thought you put into your messaging. It cares whether something feels off. It notices tone before content, effort before elegance, and intention before language.

You can overwhelm the explainer with data and still lose the sale if the decider senses pressure, confusion, or insecurity.

And once the decider checks out, no amount of logic will bring it back. You're just talking to yourself in nicer fonts.

Why Logic Feels So Good *(and Works So Poorly)*

Logic is comforting to sellers.

> It feels solid.

> It feels respectable.

> It feels like control.

Emotion, on the other hand, feels slippery and unpredictable. So we treat it like a problem to be managed rather than the engine it is.

Here's the uncomfortable Graybeard truth:

Logic does not lead decisions. It legitimizes them.

> Logic is the lawyer.

> Emotion is the judge.

> Instinct already wrote the verdict.

When people say, "I just didn't feel good about it," they are not being vague. They are being precise in a language we stopped respecting.

Smart People, Same Wiring

There's a persistent belief that smarter customers behave differently.

They don't.

They just decorate their instincts more convincingly.

Highly educated buyers still avoid discomfort.

Senior executives still trust familiarity.

Experienced professionals still react negatively to pressure.

The difference is that they can explain it afterward in a way that sounds strategic instead of human.

This leads organizations to a dangerous conclusion:

"If we just explain better, they'll decide differently."

They won't.

They'll just explain their existing decision with better vocabulary.

The Suspicion of Effort

One of the least discussed forces in selling is this:

The subconscious is suspicious of effort.

Try too hard and something tightens.

Push urgency and defenses rise.

Over-explain and trust erodes.

This is why desperation never sells well and confidence rarely needs footnotes.

The decider is exquisitely sensitive to imbalance. When the energy feels mismatched, when enthusiasm feels manufactured, when urgency feels borrowed, it steps back.

> Not loudly.
>
> Politely.
>
> Permanently.

Why Great Sellers Feel Different

Think about the best salesperson you've ever encountered.

> They probably didn't talk much.

> They didn't rush.

> They didn't chase.

They answered questions without cornering you. They allowed silence. They made it easy to leave.

That's not accidental. That's respect for how the decider works.

Great sellers don't push decisions forward.

They remove reasons to push them away.

The Quiet Mechanic of Yes

When the sale works, it doesn't feel like a win. It feels like resolution.

> Something settles.

> The tension eases.

The choice feels obvious in retrospect.

People often say, "It just made sense."

That's not logic talking.

That's relief.

The Graybeard Takeaway

If there's one thing to carry forward from this chapter, it's this:

You are never selling to a mind that wants to be convinced.

You are selling to a mind that wants to feel safe enough to decide.

Talk to that mind first.

Bring coffee.

The decider already knows what it wants.

CHAPTER 2
The Myth of the Rational Customer

Somewhere in a conference room, right now, a very serious person is saying,

"Our customer is highly rational."

This statement is usually followed by nodding, a few underlined notes, and the quiet confidence that logic is about to save the day.

It won't.

The rational customer is a comforting myth. A professional fairy tale we tell ourselves so the world feels orderly and our spreadsheets feel relevant.

Humans are not irrational.

They are pre-rational.

And that distinction matters.

Where the Myth Came From

The idea of the rational customer didn't come from psychology. It came from economics, where people are imaginary and always have perfect information, unlimited time, and an emotional range similar to a calculator.

This made modeling easier.

It did not make selling better.

When marketing borrowed that assumption, it inherited the fantasy along with the equations. Suddenly, buyers were expected to behave like neat decision trees, calmly weighing options until the optimal choice revealed itself.

Anyone who has watched a human buy a television knows this is optimistic.

What Rational Actually Looks Like

Real rationality doesn't look like deliberation. It looks like relief.

When a decision feels safe, people stop thinking about it. They don't optimize endlessly. They move on with their lives.

That's not laziness. That's efficiency.

The brain is constantly asking, Have I thought about this enough to stop thinking about it?

Selling succeeds when the answer becomes yes.

The Emotional First Draft

Every decision begins as a feeling.

Before words form, before criteria are applied, the brain produces a rough draft in emotion. Comfort or discomfort. Trust or suspicion. Interest or avoidance.

Only later does the conscious mind step in to revise.

This is why people struggle to articulate why they didn't buy. They say things like:

- "It just didn't feel right."
- "Something was off."
- "I couldn't quite put my finger on it."

Those aren't excuses. They are accurate reports from a system that doesn't speak in sentences.

Intelligence Doesn't Change the Wiring

One of the most persistent mistakes in selling is assuming that smarter audiences behave differently.

They don't.

They feel first, just like everyone else. They simply explain better afterward.

In fact, high intelligence can make this worse. It gives people more tools to justify instinctive decisions with impressive language. The conclusion doesn't change. The footnotes do.

This is why brilliant teams still make very human decisions and then spend hours explaining why they were inevitable.

Why More Information Rarely Helps

When selling stalls, the reflex response is almost always the same: add more information.

> More features.
> More proof points.
> More slides.

But information only helps if the emotional groundwork is already laid. Without that foundation, more data increases friction instead of clarity.

The rational mind can only evaluate what the emotional mind has allowed onto the table.

When something feels wrong, no amount of information fixes it. It just makes the wrongness louder.

The Illusion of Due Diligence

Due diligence feels responsible. It feels thorough. It feels safe.

But in many buying situations, it functions as permission-seeking rather than decision-making. The choice has already been made, and the process becomes a way to feel comfortable with it.

This is not deception. It's self-preservation.

People want to believe they are careful. They want to believe their decisions are defensible. Due diligence provides that comfort, even when it doesn't change the outcome.

Why We Keep Chasing Rationality

The rational customer myth persists because it flatters sellers.

It suggests that if the sale fails, the explanation must not have been clear enough or the argument not strong enough. It promises that success is just one better slide away.

Accepting the truth is harder.

It means acknowledging that selling is less about persuasion and more about design. Less about talking and more about listening. Less about cleverness and more about alignment.

Those things don't show up neatly on performance dashboards.

The Graybeard Reality Check

Here's the reality most experience eventually teaches:

People do not buy the best option.

They buy the option that feels safest to choose.

"Best" is a retrospective label. "Safe" is the real driver.

Safety doesn't mean boring. It means familiar, understandable, and non-threatening to identity.

When something threatens how people see themselves, they will reject it regardless of how rational it appears.

What Replaces the Myth

Once you let go of the rational customer myth, something better takes its place.

You stop asking:

- "How do we convince them?"

And start asking:

- What might be making this feel uncomfortable?"

- "What uncertainty haven't we addressed?

- "Where are we asking them to work too hard?"

Those questions lead to quieter, more effective selling.

The Graybeard Takeaway

The rational customer does not exist.

There are only humans trying to make good decisions with limited energy, imperfect information, and a strong desire to avoid regret.

Selling improves dramatically when you stop fighting that reality and start designing for it.

After the break, we'll look at the role emotion actually plays in decision-making and why treating it as a flaw instead of a feature has been costing businesses dearly.

The myth was useful.

The truth is more profitable.

CHAPTER 3

Emotion Is the Operating System

Most organizations treat emotion like a plug-in.

> Nice to have.

> Optional.

> Something you add at the end once the "real work" is done.

This is backwards.

Emotion is not a feature layered on top of rational thought.

Emotion is the platform everything else runs on.

> Logic doesn't lead.

> Logic loads after.

The Mistake We Keep Making

In business, emotion is often spoken about in hushed tones, as if admitting its influence might invalidate the seriousness of the enterprise.

> We talk about facts.

> We talk about performance.

> We talk about value.

And then, if we're feeling bold, we talk about emotion as a "nice enhancement."

But watch what happens when emotion is absent.

> The message becomes forgettable.

> The choice feels heavy.

> The decision stalls.

Not because the information is wrong, but because nothing is pulling it forward.

How the Brain Actually Works

The brain is not a courtroom.

It's a triage unit.

It constantly prioritizes:

- comfort over precision
- certainty over completeness
- speed over perfection

Emotion is the system that makes those trade-offs possible.

Without it, decision-making grinds to a halt. People become paralyzed, not enlightened.

This is why purely rational environments feel exhausting. The brain is forced to work in a mode it was never designed to inhabit for long.

Emotion as Efficiency

Emotion gets a bad reputation because it's associated with impulse and error. But from the brain's perspective, emotion is a labor-saving device.

It compresses experience into signals.

Trust.

Suspicion.

Relief.

Interest.

Avoidance.

These signals allow the brain to move forward without running every scenario to exhaustion.

Emotion doesn't slow decisions down.

It allows them to happen at all.

Why Fear, Familiarity, and Relief Matter So Much

Certain emotions show up in selling again and again because they solve very specific problems for the brain.

> Fear warns of risk.

> Familiarity reduces uncertainty.

> Relief signals that effort can stop.

When selling aligns with these emotions, progress feels natural. When it fights them, resistance appears.

This is why people gravitate toward brands they recognize, even when alternatives are objectively better. Familiarity lowers cognitive cost.

This is also why people describe good buying decisions as "a weight off my shoulders." That's not metaphor. That's physiology.

The False Promise of Excitement

Marketers often chase excitement, assuming it's the strongest emotional lever.

It isn't.

> Excitement attracts attention.

> Relief closes decisions.

> Excitement is forward-looking.

> Relief is resolving.

Selling that stays in excitement mode creates motion without closure. It feels stimulating but unstable.

The brain enjoys excitement briefly. It commits when it feels relief.

Emotion and Identity

One of the most powerful emotional drivers in any decision is identity.

People don't just buy products.

> They buy versions of themselves.
>
> Will this make me feel competent?
>
> Will this align with how I see myself?
>
> Will this choice embarrass me later?

These questions are emotional, not analytical, and they run constantly in the background.

Selling that threatens identity fails quietly. Selling that affirms it feels reassuring.

Why Emotion Can't Be "Added Later"

Emotion is not something you sprinkle on top of a finished argument.

If the underlying experience feels wrong, emotional language feels manipulative. If the experience feels aligned, emotion doesn't need to be mentioned at all.

This is why heartfelt language rings hollow when the environment contradicts it. The subconscious believes what it experiences, not what it's told.

The Graybeard Pattern

With enough years behind you, you start to notice a pattern.

The ideas that endure are rarely the loudest.

They are the ones that feel right quickly and continue to feel right over time.

> They don't rely on constant reinforcement.
>
> They don't require ongoing justification.
>
> They settle in. That settling is emotional.

The Graybeard Takeaway

Emotion is not the enemy of reason.

It is the reason decisions happen at all.

Selling becomes quieter and more effective when you stop treating emotion as a liability and start designing for it as the operating system it is.

In the next chapter, we'll turn to what shapes emotion before a word is spoken: context, environment, and the subtle signals that do most of the real work in selling.

The system is already running.

PART II
Context Is the Sale
(Everything Else Is Just Commentary)

By now, one uncomfortable truth should be settling in:

People don't respond to messages.

They respond to situations.

Yet most selling effort is spent polishing what to say while ignoring where, when, and how it will be received. We obsess over wording and treat context as background noise.

That's a mistake.

Context isn't the backdrop to the sale.

It is the sale.

The Graybeard Shift

Graybeards eventually stop asking, "What should we say?"

They start asking, "What is this decision sitting inside?"

Because the same message can feel reassuring in one environment and suspicious in another. The words didn't change. The context did.

Tone, timing, sequence, setting, and expectation do more persuasion than any claim you can make.

Before the Pitch Comes the Permission

Every selling moment begins with an unspoken negotiation.

> Is this worth my attention?

> Am I safe here?

Do I feel rushed, judged, or trapped?

Can I leave without consequence?

If the context answers those questions poorly, the message never lands. It doesn't matter how true it is.

Selling fails long before the pitch when permission is not quietly granted.

Environment Is an Argument

The brain is always reading the room.

It notices:

- how hard you're trying
- how much effort you're asking for
- whether urgency feels borrowed
- whether confidence feels earned

These signals arrive before language and weigh more heavily than logic ever will.

Environment argues even when you're silent.

Why Context Is Invisible Until It Breaks

Context works best when it goes unnoticed.

When it's right, nothing feels wrong.

When it's wrong, everything feels off.

That "off" feeling is not vague. It's the brain detecting friction, mismatch, or risk.

Most organizations don't measure context because it doesn't show up neatly in analytics. But customers feel it instantly.

Part II explores the quiet forces that shape decisions before anyone speaks.

We'll look at:

- how timing influences trust
- why familiarity outperforms novelty
- how environment creates or destroys permission
- and why small contextual shifts often outperform major messaging changes

This is not about manipulation.

It's about alignment.

A Graybeard Warning

Once you understand context, you'll stop blaming customers for not "getting it."

You'll see how often selling fails because the situation asked too much, too soon, or in the wrong way.

That realization changes how you design everything that comes next.

The Quiet Advantage

In a noisy world, context is your advantage.

It's harder to copy.

It's harder to fake.

And when done well, it makes selling feel effortless.

Turn the page.

The room matters more than the speech.

Chapter 4

Before the Pitch Comes the Permission

Most sales conversations fail before the first real sentence is finished.

Not because the product is wrong.

Not because the price is too high.

But because permission was never granted.

The pitch shows up uninvited.

The Silent Gatekeeper

Every buying situation has a gatekeeper, and it is not procurement, legal, or the person with the longest title.

It's the subconscious.

Before a single word is evaluated, the brain asks a quiet set of questions:

- Do I have time for this?

- Am I safe here?

- Is this going to be awkward?

- Can I disengage without penalty?

If those questions are not answered favorably, nothing else matters. The pitch can be brilliant. The logic can be flawless. The meeting can be perfectly scheduled.

The gate stays closed.

Why Attention Is a Privilege, Not a Right

Attention used to be cheap.

Now it's guarded like a scarce resource.

When sellers assume attention is owed, they trigger resistance. The subconscious notices entitlement immediately. It responds by withholding curiosity.

This is why cold pitches feel colder than ever. Not because people are unfriendly, but because they're protecting limited mental bandwidth.

Permission is not granted because you showed up.

It's granted because the situation feels respectful.

How Permission Is Actually Granted

Permission is rarely verbal. No one says, "You may now persuade me."

It shows up as:

- relaxed posture

- slower speech

- longer pauses

- genuine questions

- silence that isn't uncomfortable

These are signals that the gate has opened, just enough.

Push too early and it slams shut.

The Cost of Premature Persuasion

Premature persuasion is one of the most common selling mistakes.

It happens when:

- urgency is introduced before trust

- features appear before relevance

- certainty is asserted before understanding

The subconscious interprets this as risk.

Why are they rushing?

Why are they explaining so much?

Why do they seem invested in my decision before I am?

These questions don't sound dramatic, but they are fatal.

The Graybeard Test

Here's a simple test seasoned sellers use, often without realizing it:

If the buyer hasn't asked a question yet, you're too early.

Questions are permission in motion. They signal that the buyer's brain has shifted from defense to exploration.

Until then, your job is not to explain.

Your job is to settle the room.

How to Set the Room

Setting the room is quiet work.

It involves:

- acknowledging uncertainty instead of hiding it
- allowing exits instead of blocking them
- matching pace instead of imposing it
- saying less instead of more

This feels counterintuitive in a culture that rewards activity. But stillness builds more trust than motion at the wrong time.

Why Silence Works

Silence is often mistaken for weakness.

In reality, it signals confidence.

Only someone who is not desperate for an outcome can afford to pause. The subconscious reads that immediately.

Silence gives the other brain space to arrive at its own conclusions without interference.

When people reach decisions themselves, they defend them fiercely.

Permission in Digital Spaces

Permission matters just as much online.

A cluttered website screams impatience.

A popup before value feels grabby.

An email that demands attention without earning it gets ignored.

Digital environments either grant permission or revoke it instantly.

Design is a conversation long before copy is read.

The Graybeard Takeaway

Selling does not begin with persuasion.

It begins with permission.

If you learn to recognize when permission has been granted and, more importantly, when it has not, selling becomes calmer and far more effective.

After the break, we'll explore how environment itself argues on your behalf and why context often does the heavy lifting while words take the credit.

The gate matters more than the pitch.

CHAPTER 5

Environment Beats Argument

If logic closed sales, libraries would be cash registers.

They are not.

People don't decide inside arguments.

They decide inside environments.

And environments are always talking, whether you are or not.

The Argument You're Not Making

Every selling situation contains two arguments.

The one you prepared.

And the one the environment is making on your behalf.

The second one is louder.

It speaks through:

- layout
- pace
- effort required
- clarity or clutter
- how trapped or free someone feels

This argument begins before the meeting starts, before the website loads fully, before the first sentence leaves your mouth.

By the time you speak, the subconscious has already formed an opinion about whether you should be believed.

Why Better Arguments Rarely Win

When selling stalls, the instinctive response is to sharpen the argument.

More proof.

More data.

More explanation.

But arguments only work when the environment is already friendly. In hostile or confusing environments, arguments sound like pressure.

You can't logic your way out of a situation problem.

If the room feels rushed, your certainty feels suspicious.

If the website feels cluttered, your message feels desperate.

If the process feels heavy, your value feels theoretical.

The Brain Is a Context Detector

The subconscious doesn't evaluate claims in isolation. It reads patterns.

Is this easy to understand?

Does this feel familiar?

Is the effort proportional to the reward?

Does this match what I expected?

When those answers align, the brain relaxes. When they don't, it resists, even if the offer is good.

This resistance is not stubbornness. It's self-defense.

How Environment Creates Trust

Trust doesn't come from statements.

It comes from coherence.

When everything fits together, the brain stops looking for danger. When something feels out of place, it starts searching for motives.

Consistency in tone, design, timing, and behavior creates a sense of inevitability. The decision feels less like a leap and more like a step.

That feeling closes more sales than confidence ever will.

Effort Is a Signal

The amount of effort you ask for is part of the argument.

> Long forms.

> Complex steps.

> Dense explanations.

Each one whispers, This might be work.

The subconscious is allergic to unnecessary effort. It doesn't hate effort entirely. It hates wasted effort.

When effort feels justified, people lean in. When it feels arbitrary, they disappear.

Why Simple Often Wins

Simple does not mean shallow.

Simple means the brain doesn't have to work to feel oriented.

> Clarity reduces risk.

> Familiarity reduces fear.

> Predictability reduces doubt.

This is why processes that feel obvious outperform those that feel impressive. The brain prefers the known path over the clever detour.

The Graybeard Lesson from the Field

Graybeards eventually notice something unsettling.

The most effective selling environments rarely feel like selling environments at all.

> They feel calm.

> They feel respectful.

> They feel easy to leave.

That last one matters.

Nothing triggers suspicion faster than the feeling of being trapped. Freedom increases trust. Paradoxically, the easier it is to walk away, the more comfortable people become staying.

Digital Environments Count More Than Ever

Online, environment is the experience.

> Navigation is tone.

> Load time is confidence.

> Design is intention.

A chaotic interface undermines the most carefully written message. A calm one allows even imperfect copy to land.

People don't blame the environment. They blame the offer.

The Graybeard Takeaway

You don't win by making better arguments.

You win by making better environments.

If the environment supports the decision, words become confirmation instead of persuasion.

In the next chapter, we'll explore why familiarity is such a powerful force and how "new" often loses to "recognizable" long before features are compared.

The room always votes first.

CHAPTER 6

The Power of Familiarity

When people say they want something new, what they usually mean is recognizably better.

They want improvement without uncertainty. Progress without embarrassment. Novelty that doesn't require a user manual or an apology.

This is the power of familiarity.

Why the Brain Loves What It Recognizes

The brain is a pattern-recognition machine. It scans constantly, asking one question over and over:

Have I seen something like this before?

When the answer is yes, the brain relaxes. Familiarity reduces risk, lowers effort, and speeds decisions. It doesn't guarantee a sale, but it grants access to consideration.

This is why the unfamiliar is not evaluated fairly. It is evaluated cautiously.

Not because it's bad.

Because it's unknown.

The Comfort of "I Know This"

Familiarity doesn't have to mean old.

It can show up as:

- a recognizable structure
- expected language
- a familiar sequence
- a known metaphor
- a trusted reference point

These cues tell the brain, You're on known ground.

Once that happens, people are willing to explore differences.

Without it, they retreat.

The Cost of Being Too New

Innovation is intoxicating to sellers. It feels bold, brave, and differentiating.

To the buyer's brain, it often feels like work.

Too much novelty forces the brain into learning mode, and learning mode is effortful. Effort raises risk. Risk slows decisions.

This is why groundbreaking ideas often fail quietly while incremental improvements succeed loudly.

The brain doesn't reward originality.

It rewards usability.

Why Familiarity Beats Excitement

Excitement grabs attention. Familiarity earns trust.

Excitement says, Look at this.

Familiarity says, You know how this works.

When forced to choose, the brain will trade excitement for certainty almost every time.

This is why products described as "the Uber of" or "the Netflix for" something new gain traction faster. They borrow familiarity to lower the entry cost.

Familiarity and Identity

Familiar choices protect identity.

People don't want to feel foolish, out of place, or behind. Familiar options provide cover. They allow people to say, Others like me choose this.

That social reassurance matters more than we like to admit.

Selling that ignores this dimension asks buyers to take emotional risks they didn't sign up for.

The Familiarity Paradox

Here's the paradox:

The more innovative your offering, the more familiar the presentation needs to be.

Truly new ideas require extra scaffolding. They must be wrapped in recognizable patterns or they never get the chance to be evaluated.

This is why disruptive technologies often look boring at first and revolutionary only in hindsight.

How Familiarity Shows Up in Design

Familiarity is communicated through consistency.

> Predictable navigation.

> Expected interactions.

> Clear progression.

When people know where they are and what comes next, anxiety drops. Decision-making accelerates.

Confusion kills momentum faster than skepticism.

The Graybeard Shortcut

Graybeards know this instinctively:

If you have to explain how something works before explaining why it matters, you've already lost half the room.

Familiarity clears the runway so meaning can take off.

The Graybeard Takeaway

People don't resist change.

They resist uncertainty.

Familiarity is the bridge between the two.

Tomorrow, we'll look at how desire is actually unresolved tension and why people buy to stop thinking, not to start dreaming.

The brain likes new roads best when they look well traveled.

Desire, Tension, and the Quiet Yes

By the time someone reaches for their wallet, clicks the button, or signs their name, they are not chasing a thing.

They are escaping a feeling.

This is where many explanations of selling drift off course. They talk about aspiration, acquisition, and advantage, as if people buy to add something new to their lives.

More often, they buy to make something stop.

The Graybeard Reframe

Graybeards learn this the long way, usually after watching beautifully positioned products gather dust while less impressive ones move effortlessly.

The difference isn't desire.

It's tension.

Desire is not a hunger for more.

It's discomfort with the current state.

People don't wake up wanting solutions. They wake up wanting relief.

What Tension Feels Like

Tension shows up as:
- uncertainty
- doubt
- inefficiency
- embarrassment
- frustration
- the quiet sense that something isn't quite right

It's not always dramatic. Often it's subtle, persistent, and exhausting.

The brain doesn't rush to fix tension immediately. It tolerates it until the cost of tolerating it exceeds the cost of change.

That crossing point is the sale.

Why Features Don't Resolve Tension

Features describe capability.

Tension describes experience.

Selling fails when it explains what something does instead of what it ends.

People rarely buy because a feature exists. They buy because a problem finally has a name and an exit.

Until tension is recognized, no offer feels relevant.

Relief Is the Real Product

This is the quiet truth behind every successful sale:

What people purchase is not the product.

It's the feeling that comes after the decision.

> Relief.
>
> Reassurance.
>
> Closure.

Those feelings are the real value, and they live beyond the transaction.

Part III explores selling at the moment it actually happens.

We'll look at:

- how tension forms and lingers
- why naming it matters more than solving it immediately
- how friction removal closes more sales than persuasion ever could
- and why the "yes" feels inevitable when done right

This is where selling stops looking like selling and starts looking like understanding.

A Graybeard Warning

If you're uncomfortable talking about emotion, tension, and relief, this section may feel unsteady.

That's normal.

We're moving away from tidy models and into lived experience. The kind that doesn't fit neatly into dashboards but shows up reliably in outcomes.

The Quiet Promise

When tension is understood and respected, selling becomes calm.

> No pressure.

> No urgency.

> No theatrics.

Just a quiet moment when the right decision reveals itself.

Notebooks open.

The tension has already been waiting.

Chapter 7

Desire Is Unresolved Tension

People don't wake up wanting products.

They wake up wanting something to stop.

> The noise.

> The uncertainty.

> The inefficiency.

The low-grade frustration that hums in the background of their day like an appliance that never quite shuts off.

We call that desire.

It isn't longing.

It's irritation with the status quo.

The Marketing Romance We Tell Ourselves

Marketing loves to frame desire as aspiration.

> Better life.

> Better future.

> Better version of you.

That story is appealing, but incomplete.

> Aspiration attracts attention.

> Tension drives action.

People admire what they aspire to.

> They buy what resolves discomfort.

This is why so many "inspiring" campaigns are memorable and ineffective. They make people feel good without making them move.

How Tension Forms

Tension forms when reality and expectation drift apart.

> Something should be easier by now.

> Something shouldn't still be this annoying.

> Something feels out of step with who I think I am.

The brain tolerates small mismatches for a long time. It adapts. It works around them.

> But unresolved tension accumulates.

And when it does, the brain starts scanning for exits.

The Problem with Problem Statements

Here's a subtle but important distinction.

> Not every problem creates tension.

> Not every tension feels like a problem.

People don't act on what you tell them is broken.

> They act on what they already feel is heavy.

Selling often fails because it introduces a problem the buyer hasn't emotionally acknowledged yet.

When that happens, the pitch feels irrelevant or insulting.

Why Naming Tension Matters More Than Solving It

The most powerful selling moments often happen before a solution is fully presented.

They happen when someone says, "Yes, that's exactly it."

That recognition creates relief on its own. It tells the buyer they are understood. That their frustration is valid. That they are not imagining it.

Once tension is named accurately, the solution feels secondary.

Misname it, and the solution never lands.

Tension and Identity

Some of the strongest tensions are tied to identity.

I shouldn't still be struggling with this.

Someone like me should have figured this out by now.

This makes me look unprepared, behind, or careless.

These tensions are rarely spoken aloud, but they exert enormous pressure.

Selling that ignores identity tension stays on the surface. Selling that respects it feels personal without being intrusive.

The Tolerance Threshold

People don't act at the first sign of tension.

They act when the effort of living with it exceeds the effort of changing.

This is why timing matters so much in selling. Catch someone before the threshold, and the offer feels premature. Catch them after, and it feels obvious.

Great selling recognizes where someone is on that curve.

Why Discounts Rarely Create Desire

Lowering price doesn't resolve tension.

It changes the math, not the feeling.

If the tension isn't acknowledged, a discount feels like a distraction or, worse, a signal that something might be wrong.

When tension is clear, price becomes secondary.

The Graybeard Observation

Graybeards notice that the best closers are often the best listeners.

They don't rush to solutions. They let tension breathe. They allow silence after naming it.

That pause is not empty. It's where decisions begin to form.

The Graybeard Takeaway

Desire is not about wanting more.

It's about wanting less of what's weighing on you.

If you learn to recognize unresolved tension and name it with accuracy and respect, selling becomes less about pushing and more about timing.

In the next chapter, we'll explore why selling works best when it feels like friction removal and why ease closes more deals than excitement ever will.

The tension tells you when it's time.

Chapter 8
Selling Is Friction Removal

Most selling fails because it tries to add value.

That sounds reasonable.

It's also incomplete.

What actually moves decisions forward is not the addition of something new, but the removal of something old.

>Confusion.

>Effort.

>Risk.

>Doubt.

Selling works when those disappear.

The Myth of Adding More

Business culture loves accumulation.

>More features.

>More options.

>More proof.

>More urgency.

We treat selling like stacking bricks, assuming that if we build high enough, someone will climb aboard.

But every addition carries a cost.

Each new option adds decision weight.

Each new explanation adds effort.

Each new claim adds something to evaluate.

The brain doesn't want more.

It wants easier.

What Friction Actually Is

Friction is anything that makes a decision feel heavier than it needs to be.

It shows up as:

- uncle ar next steps
- unexpected effort
- social risk
- cognitive overload
- fear of regret

Friction doesn't announce itself loudly. It whispers. It feels like hesitation, delay, or "I'll get back to this later."

Later is where many good offers go to die.

The Brain's Efficiency Mandate

The brain is constantly balancing effort against reward.

When effort feels disproportionate, even valuable opportunities are rejected. Not consciously. Automatically.

This is why small inconveniences derail big intentions. The brain conserves energy ruthlessly.

Selling that ignores this reality feels tone-deaf.

Why Ease Builds Trust

Ease is not laziness.

Ease signals competence.

When something feels simple, the subconscious reads it as well-designed, well-understood, and safe.

When something feels complicated, the subconscious wonders why.

Ease doesn't mean hiding complexity. It means managing it on behalf of the buyer.

The Power of Removing One Thing

You don't have to remove everything.

Removing one key friction point can unlock momentum.

One unclear step clarified.

One risk acknowledged and softened.

One unnecessary choice eliminated.

These changes often outperform sweeping campaigns because they operate where decisions actually stall.

Friction Hides in Processes

Many selling problems live inside the process, not the message.

Too many steps.

Too many approvals.

Too much waiting.

Each delay gives doubt time to grow.

The longer a decision sits unresolved, the heavier it feels.

The Graybeard Lesson on Momentum

Graybeards know momentum is fragile.

It doesn't need hype.

It needs continuity.

Every pause is a chance for tension to dissipate or turn into avoidance.

Selling that respects momentum focuses on making the next step feel light.

When Friction Is Necessary

Not all friction is bad.

Some friction signals seriousness.

Some effort signals commitment.

The key is intentionality.

Friction that feels purposeful builds trust. Friction that feels arbitrary kills it.

The brain can tell the difference.

The Graybeard Takeaway

Selling is not about pushing people forward.

It's about clearing the path.

When friction is removed, decisions don't feel forced. They feel natural.

In the next chapter, we'll look at the moment when "yes" stops feeling like a choice and starts feeling inevitable.

Ease is persuasive.

Chapter 9

When Yes Becomes Inevitable

The moment of yes is rarely dramatic.

There is no internal drumroll.

> No triumphant music.

> No flash of certainty.

What there is, more often than not, is a quiet sense that there is nothing left to resolve.

That's inevitability.

The Myth of the Close

Selling lore is obsessed with "the close."

> Techniques.

> Signals.

> Lines to deliver at precisely the right moment.

This obsession comes from misunderstanding where decisions actually happen.

If you are trying to create the yes at the end, you already missed it.

The close does not cause the decision.

It reveals it.

What Inevitability Feels Like

Inevitability feels boring in the best possible way.

> No tension.

> No debate.

> No second-guessing.

The brain stops scanning for alternatives because it no longer sees a reason to.

People describe this moment as:

- "This just makes sense."
- "I don't see a reason not to."
- "Let's do it."

Those phrases sound casual because the work is already done.

The Quiet Checklist Is Complete

Before inevitability arrives, the subconscious runs through its checklist.

Is the risk acceptable?

Is the effort reasonable?

Do I trust the source?

Does this fit who I am?

Can I explain this later?

When each box is checked, even loosely, resistance dissolves.

Not because of persuasion.

Because there is nothing left to push against.

Why Pressure Breaks the Moment

Pressure at this stage is especially dangerous.

It introduces new tension right as the old tension is resolving.

The subconscious reacts immediately:

Why are they rushing now?

What do they know that I don't?

That suspicion can undo everything.

This is why great sellers slow down just as things start moving.

The Role of Silence

Silence is not empty during inevitability.

It's active.

It gives the decision space to surface without interference. It allows the buyer to hear their own internal conclusion.

Talking through that moment often interrupts it.

The instinct to fill silence is one of the most expensive habits in selling.

When the Yes Is Borrowed

Not all yeses are equal.

A borrowed yes comes from pressure, urgency, or social obligation. It closes quickly and unravels just as fast.

An inevitable yes comes from internal alignment. It sticks.

You can feel the difference immediately.

One feels tense.

The other feels settled.

The Graybeard Signal

Graybeards stop listening for verbal cues.

They watch for:

- relaxed shoulders
- slower speech
- fewer questions
- curiosity about next steps instead of justification

These are signs the decision has already landed.

The role of the seller now is simple: don't disrupt it.

Why This Feels Uncomfortable at First

Allowing inevitability requires restraint.

> It means trusting the process.

> It means not grabbing credit.

> It means letting the buyer feel ownership.

That restraint feels risky to inexperienced sellers. It feels like losing control.

It isn't.

It's professionalism.

The Graybeard Takeaway

The yes you want arrives when everything unnecessary has been removed.

> You don't close it.

> You recognize it.

In the next class, we'll look at trust, consistency, and why the subconscious distrusts effort even when intentions are good.

When yes feels inevitable, your job is to step aside.

Trust Is Built Quietly

(And Lost Loudly)

By the time a decision feels inevitable, trust has already done its work.

Not the kind of trust that comes from slogans or promises, but the quieter kind that forms when nothing feels wrong enough to stop moving forward.

Trust is not a statement.

It's an absence.

> An absence of friction.

> An absence of suspicion.

> An absence of reasons to hesitate.

The Graybeard Observation

Graybeards learn, often the hard way, that trust cannot be accelerated.

> You can demand it.

> You can request it.

> You can talk about it endlessly.

None of that works.

Trust emerges when behavior, environment, and tone line up over time. It is cumulative, fragile, and mercilessly honest.

One off-note doesn't just weaken trust.

It redraws the entire picture.

Why Effort Backfires

Modern selling often mistakes effort for commitment.

More follow-ups.

More urgency.

More reassurance.

But effort reads differently to the subconscious.

It asks a dangerous question:

Why do they need to work this hard?

Confidence doesn't announce itself.

Credibility doesn't chase.

When effort becomes visible, trust quietly slips out the side door.

Signals Speak Louder Than Claims

People don't trust what you say about yourself.

They trust what you do when no one is asking.

Design choices.

Consistency.

Restraint.

What you don't say.

These signals are read continuously and believed more than any declaration ever could be.

Part IV explores the unglamorous mechanics of trust.

We'll look at:

- why signals beat statements every time

- how consistency compounds credibility

- why overselling feels like insecurity

- and how restraint outperforms enthusiasm in the long run

This is the part of selling that rarely gets applause but quietly determines outcomes.

A Graybeard Warning

Trust work is boring on spreadsheets.

It doesn't spike metrics.

It doesn't produce viral moments.

It produces longevity.

If you're looking for fast wins, this section may feel slow. If you're building something meant to last, it's essential.

The Quiet Advantage

In a world trained to doubt, trust is the real differentiator.

Not because it's flashy, but because it's rare.

Turn the page.

Nothing sells like consistency.

CHAPTER 10
Signals Beat Statements

Trust is not built by saying the word trust.

In fact, that's often when it starts leaking.

Statements ask to be believed.

Signals simply are.

The subconscious knows the difference.

The Problem with Saying the Quiet Part Out Loud

The moment you say, "Trust us," the brain asks a question it wasn't planning to ask:

Why do they need to say that?

The same thing happens with:

- "We really care."
- "Customer-first."
- "Best-in-class."
- "Industry-leading."

These statements are not lies.

They're just loud.

And loud draws scrutiny.

The subconscious treats self-declared virtue the way a mechanic treats a car with a fresh coat of paint and no service records. It looks closer, not kinder.

What Signals Actually Are

Signals are information without commentary.

They show up in:

- how consistent things feel
- how predictable the experience is
- how much effort is required
- how calmly problems are handled
- how little drama surrounds the process

Signals don't persuade.

They accumulate.

Over time, they create a pattern the brain recognizes as safe.

Why Signals Work Better Than Claims

Claims require evaluation.

Signals bypass it.

A claim says, Believe me.

A signal says, Notice this.

The subconscious prefers noticing.

It trusts what it can observe repeatedly more than what it is told once, no matter how confidently.

This is why a single bad experience can outweigh ten good testimonials. The signal changed.

Consistency Is the Loudest Signal

Consistency is boring. That's why it works.

Same tone.

Same pacing.

Same expectations met over and over again.

Consistency reduces vigilance. When nothing changes unexpectedly, the brain stops scanning for danger.

This is also why inconsistency is so expensive. It forces the brain back into alert mode.

People rarely say, "I stopped trusting them because they were inconsistent."

They say, "Something felt off."

That's the signal talking.

The Signal of Restraint

One of the strongest trust signals is restraint.

Not saying everything you could.

Not pushing every advantage.

Not filling every silence.

Restraint suggests confidence. It implies you don't need to extract agreement immediately.

The subconscious reads this as strength.

Desperation has a smell. Restraint does not.

Design Is a Statement You Don't Control

Design signals intention whether you like it or not.

Clutter signals urgency or insecurity.

Simplicity signals clarity.

Over-polish can signal hiding.

Under-care can signal neglect.

People don't critique design consciously most of the time. They absorb it.

And once absorbed, it shapes how everything else is interpreted.

How Signals Are Lost

Trust is rarely destroyed by a single failure.

It erodes through contradiction.

When what you say and what you do don't match, the brain believes the behavior and discounts the words.

This is why apologies without change feel hollow. The statement arrives, but the signal never does.

The Graybeard Pattern

Graybeards eventually stop crafting persuasive language and start auditing signals.

They ask:

- Where are we asking people to work too hard?
- Where are we inconsistent without realizing it?
- Where are we explaining instead of fixing?

They know that the fastest way to rebuild trust is not to speak differently, but to behave differently.

The Graybeard Takeaway

If you want to know what people actually believe about you, don't listen to what they say.

Watch what they expect.

Signals shape expectations.

Statements try to manage them.

Selling becomes quieter and more effective when you stop talking about trust and start designing for it.

In the next chapter, we'll look at why consistency compounds over time and why brands don't fail loudly. They drift.

Signals never stop speaking.

CHAPTER 11
Consistency Is the Brand

Ask most organizations what their brand is, and you'll get a paragraph.

Ask customers, and you'll get a feeling.

That feeling isn't created by mission statements or taglines. It's created by repetition.

Brand is not what you say once.

It's what you do every time.

Why Consistency Feels Boring Internally

Inside an organization, consistency feels dull.

The same messages.

The same tone.

The same guardrails.

People crave novelty. They want to refresh, rebrand, and reinvent. They worry about looking stale.

Customers feel the opposite.

They don't want surprise.

They want reliability.

What feels repetitive internally feels reassuring externally.

The Subconscious Reward of Predictability

Predictability lowers cognitive load.

When people know what to expect, they stop scanning for risk. They move faster. They trust more easily.

This is why the brain relaxes when patterns repeat. It recognizes safety.

Brands that change direction frequently force customers to re-evaluate constantly. That reevaluation feels like work.

Work erodes trust.

Consistency Beats Intensity

A single powerful moment does less than a hundred ordinary ones done right.

Intensity spikes attention.

Consistency builds belief.

This is why short-lived campaigns rarely create loyalty. They excite and then vanish.

Trust grows through accumulation.

The Cost of Inconsistency

Inconsistency doesn't announce itself as failure.

It shows up as hesitation.

As delayed decisions.

As quieter conversations.

People rarely complain about inconsistency. They simply stop engaging.

The brand didn't offend them.

It exhausted them.

Internal Alignment Shows Up Externally

Consistency requires alignment inside the organization.

When departments interpret the brand differently, the experience fractures. Each interaction feels slightly out of sync.

Customers may not articulate the issue, but they feel it.

Fragmentation reads as unreliability.

Why Rebrands Often Fail

Rebrands are seductive.

They promise renewal, relevance, and fresh energy.

They also risk erasing accumulated trust.

When a brand changes faster than its behavior, confusion follows. Familiarity is lost, and the brain re-enters evaluation mode.

Unless something is truly broken, consistency usually outperforms reinvention.

The Graybeard Observation

Graybeards know that strong brands age well.

They evolve slowly.

They keep their core intact.

They change the edges, not the center.

They resist the urge to chase trends at the expense of recognition.

The Graybeard Takeaway

Brand is not a campaign.

It's a pattern.

Consistency turns ordinary experiences into trusted ones. It allows people to decide quickly because they've decided many times before.

In the next class, we'll explore why trying too hard often signals insecurity and how overselling quietly undermines everything you've built.

Repetition is reputation.

CHAPTER 12
The Danger of Trying Too Hard

Nothing makes the subconscious more uneasy than visible effort.

Not work.

Effort.

Work feels grounded.

Effort feels needy.

The difference is subtle, and the brain detects it instantly.

When Energy Feels Mismatched

Trying too hard shows up as imbalance.

Too many follow-ups.

Too much urgency.

Too much reassurance.

The subconscious response is automatic:

Why are they pushing this?

What's making them nervous?

Even when intentions are good, the signal is wrong.

Overselling Is a Confession

Overselling is rarely strategic.

It's reactive.

It happens when confidence drops and activity increases to compensate. The more uncertain the seller feels, the louder the message becomes.

The buyer's brain hears this clearly.

Confidence doesn't explain itself.

Insecurity does.

The Volume Problem

Raising volume is a natural response to fear.

But louder does not mean clearer.

It means something wasn't working earlier.

This is why urgency language backfires when it's not earned. Scarcity only works when it's real. Manufactured pressure smells artificial because it is.

Why Silence Feels Risky

Silence feels dangerous to people who equate motion with progress.

But silence is often the moment when trust consolidates.

When you stop talking, you allow the buyer to hear their own thinking. Interrupting that process resets it.

The instinct to fill space is human.

The discipline to leave it empty is professional.

The Subconscious Penalty for Effort

Effort creates debt.

Every push demands a response. Every follow-up asks for justification.

Eventually, the easiest response becomes avoidance.

This is how good opportunities quietly fade without explanation.

How Restraint Builds Authority

Restraint is the inverse of effort.

It signals:

- confidence

- patience

- independence from the outcome

People trust those who don't need them.

This doesn't mean indifference. It means stability.

The Graybeard Pattern

Graybeards stop chasing outcomes.

We focus on making interactions feel balanced.

We know that when energy is right, progress happens naturally. When it's wrong, no tactic will fix it.

The Graybeard Takeaway

Trying harder is rarely the answer.

Trying quieter often is.

When you feel the urge to push, pause. The work you should be doing likely comes earlier in the process.

In the next class, we'll explore how to design selling that doesn't feel like selling at all.

Effort is loud. Confidence is calm.

Selling Without Selling

If you've made it this far, something should feel different.

Not louder.

Not more aggressive.

Quieter.

That's the point.

Part V is not about new tactics. It's about what remains after everything unnecessary has been removed.

The Graybeard Realization

Graybeards eventually discover that the most effective selling doesn't look like selling.

There's no chase.

No pressure.

No performance.

Just a calm alignment between what someone needs and what's being offered.

When that alignment is real, persuasion becomes irrelevant.

What Selling Without Selling Means

It doesn't mean doing nothing.

It means designing experiences so well that the decision emerges naturally.

It means:

- removing friction before it's noticed
- earning trust before it's tested

- allowing familiarity to do its work
- letting relief close the deal

Selling without selling is intentional invisibility.

Why This Feels Counterintuitive

Most people were trained to associate selling with activity.

Talking.

Explaining.

Following up.

Letting go of those habits feels risky, especially in environments that reward visible effort.

But visible effort is not the same as effectiveness.

Part V brings everything together.

We'll look at:
- how to make the right choice feel obvious
- how to design for real humans, not ideal ones
- how quiet strategy outperforms noise in the long run

This is not about becoming passive. It's about becoming precise.

The Graybeard Advantage

Quiet selling compounds.

It builds reputation.

It builds referrals.

It builds longevity.

It trades short-term wins for sustained momentum.

In a world addicted to volume, restraint is a competitive advantage.

The Quiet Promise

When selling is done right, people don't feel persuaded.

They feel understood.

Turn the page.

There's nothing left to push.

CHAPTER 13
Make the Right Choice Feel Obvious

The goal of selling is not to convince.

It's to remove enough friction that the decision no longer feels like a decision.

When the right choice feels obvious, action follows without drama.

Obvious Is Not Simple-Minded

"Obvious" is often mistaken for "dumbed down."

It isn't.

Obvious means the brain doesn't have to work to understand what comes next. It recognizes the path and sees no reason to resist it.

> Obvious feels calm.
> Obvious feels proportionate.
> Obvious feels safe.

That feeling is engineered, not accidental.

Why Choice Feels Heavy

Choice becomes heavy when:

- too many options compete
- criteria aren't clear
- trade-offs feel risky
- the consequences feel irreversible

The brain doesn't enjoy optimizing. It enjoys settling.

When selling adds choices instead of resolving them, hesitation grows.

The Power of Fewer Doors

Every option you offer is a door someone has to evaluate.

Too many doors slow movement.

This is why guided choice outperforms open menus. The brain relaxes when someone competent has already narrowed the field.

Curation is kindness.

Framing the Path Forward

Making a choice feel obvious is often about framing sequence, not outcome.

> What happens first?

> What happens next?

> What can wait?

When people see a clear path, anxiety drops. The decision becomes about starting, not finishing.

Selling succeeds when the first step feels light.

Removing the Need to Defend the Choice

One of the brain's quiet concerns is social.

Will I have to explain this later?

When a choice aligns with common sense, familiar patterns, or widely accepted norms, it feels defensible.

Obvious choices require fewer explanations.

Why Obvious Beats Clever

Clever attracts attention.

Obvious earns commitment.

Clever asks to be admired.

Obvious asks to be used.

In selling, admiration without action is failure dressed well.

The Graybeard Shortcut

Graybeards ask a simple question:

If I were distracted, tired, and mildly skeptical, would this still make sense?

If the answer is no, the design isn't finished.

The Graybeard Takeaway

Selling works best when people don't feel smart for choosing you.

They feel comfortable.

When the right choice feels obvious, the yes doesn't need encouragement.

In the next chapter, we'll look at how designing for real humans, not ideal ones, changes everything.

Obvious is earned.

CHAPTER 14

Design for the Human You Actually Get

Most selling fails because it's designed for an imaginary customer.

>Attentive.

>Patient.

>Well-rested.

>Eager to evaluate options.

That person does not exist.

The customer you actually get is distracted, busy, mildly skeptical, and carrying a mental to-do list that would make a project manager cry.

Design for that human.

The Myth of the Ideal Buyer

In planning rooms, buyers are calm and cooperative. They read carefully. They consider thoughtfully. They appreciate nuance.

In real life, buyers are:

- interrupted
- multitasking
- emotionally preoccupied
- conserving energy

This is not a moral failing. It's reality.

Selling that ignores this reality asks too much and gets too little.

Cognitive Budget Is Limited

Every decision spends mental energy.

When that budget is depleted, people default to:

- postponement

- avoidance

- familiar choices

Selling that demands focus without offering relief loses by default.

This is why complexity kills momentum even when value is high.

Why "More Control" Often Backfires

Giving people unlimited control feels respectful.

It's often exhausting.

Too many choices force people into evaluation mode. Evaluation mode burns energy quickly.

Guidance reduces fatigue.

Structure reduces anxiety.

Design that feels helpful is design that quietly decides with the buyer.

The Reality of Partial Attention

Selling assumes attention.

Reality offers fragments.

People skim.

They miss details.

They misunderstand.

This is not carelessness. It's modern life.

Design that survives partial attention wins.

Error-Tolerant Design Builds Trust

People don't want perfection.

They want forgiveness.

Clear recovery paths, easy corrections, and graceful exits signal safety. The brain relaxes when it knows mistakes aren't fatal.

Fear of irreversible error stops decisions cold.

The Graybeard Test, Revisited

Graybeards ask:

- Where can someone get confused?
- Where might they hesitate?
- Where are we asking them to remember too much?

They design around those weak points.

Selling improves when you assume distraction instead of attention.

The Graybeard Takeaway

The smartest selling strategy is empathy expressed as design.

> Not ideal empathy.

> Practical empathy.

Design for the human you actually get, and decisions start making themselves.

In the final class, we'll look at why quiet strategy outlasts noise and how to build something that keeps working when the shouting stops.

Reality beats theory.

CHAPTER 15
Quiet Strategy in a Noisy World

The world did not get noisier by accident.

Noise is what happens when everyone is trying to be heard at the same time, using the same tools, chasing the same attention, measuring success by volume instead of effect.

Selling followed suit.

> More emails.

> More urgency.

> More content.

> More reminders that something is "ending soon,"
> even when it isn't.

And in response, people learned to tune out.

Noise Stops Working Before It Stops Being Used

One of the strange things about noise is that it lingers long after it stops being effective.

Organizations keep turning the volume knob because lowering it feels like surrender. Silence feels risky. Quiet feels like absence.

But the human brain has adapted.

> It filters.

> It skips.

> It scrolls.

> It deletes without opening.

Noise doesn't persuade anymore.

It just announces itself as noise.

What Quiet Actually Does

Quiet does not compete for attention.

It waits for relevance.

Quiet strategy assumes that timing matters more than frequency and that clarity matters more than cleverness. It doesn't chase every moment. It shows up when tension already exists.

Quiet respects the buyer's mental state instead of trying to override it.

That respect is felt.

Why Quiet Feels Stronger Now

In a loud environment, quiet feels intentional.

> It signals confidence.

> It signals patience.

> It signals that you don't need to grab.

The subconscious notices this immediately.

When everything else is shouting, calm reads as authority.

The Long Game Most People Quit Too Early

Quiet strategy doesn't spike metrics overnight.

> It compounds.

> It builds familiarity instead of flash.

> It earns trust instead of borrowing it.

> It creates decisions that stick instead of yeses that evaporate.

This is why quiet strategies are often abandoned prematurely. They require restraint in a culture that rewards motion.

Graybeards stay the course.

What Quiet Strategy Looks Like in Practice

It looks like:

- fewer messages, better timed
- clearer paths, fewer choices
- consistency instead of reinvention
- patience instead of pressure

It looks like designing experiences that don't demand attention but reward it when given.

The Hidden Advantage of Quiet

Quiet selling creates space.

Space for thought.

Space for recognition.

Space for the buyer to feel ownership of the decision.

Ownership is what turns customers into advocates and transactions into relationships.

You can't force that.

You can only allow it.

The Graybeard Ending

After enough years, patterns become obvious.

Loud strategies burn bright and fade fast.

Quiet strategies work slowly and endure.

The best selling doesn't feel like selling because it isn't trying to win.

It's trying to fit.

And when something fits, it doesn't need to be announced.

The Final Graybeard Takeaway

Selling has not become harder.

It has become more honest.

The quiet truth is that people still decide the same way they always have. What's changed is their tolerance for being pushed.

If you remove friction, respect attention, and design for real humans, selling becomes simpler.

Not easier.

Simpler.

When the noise stops working, quiet is not a retreat.

It's the advantage.

The Sale You Never Had to Make

The best sales leave no evidence.

>No pressure marks.

>No raised voices.

>No clever lines that get quoted later.

Just a decision that feels settled enough to stop thinking about.

What Quiet Success Looks Like

When selling is done well, no one says, "I was sold."

They say:

- "It just made sense."
- "It felt right."
- "It was the obvious choice."

Those phrases are not compliments. They are confirmations.

They mean the work happened where it was supposed to happen and stayed out of sight.

The Graybeard Perspective

With enough years behind you, you stop chasing moments.

You stop looking for the perfect pitch, the flawless close, the line that finally unlocks everything.

You start paying attention to patterns.

>Where do people relax?

>Where do they hesitate?

>Where do they quietly move forward?

Those signals are more honest than words.

What You Stop Doing

Quiet selling changes your behavior.

You stop:

- overexplaining
- rushing
- filling silence
- mistaking activity for progress

You stop trying to win and start trying to fit.

And fitting lasts longer.

What You Start Doing

You start:

- designing for ease
- respecting attention
- trusting familiarity
- removing friction early
- letting decisions arrive on their own schedule

These are not dramatic moves.

They are durable ones.

Why This Works Beyond Selling

This way of thinking doesn't stop at sales.

It shows up in leadership.

In teaching.

In relationships.

People move toward what feels safe, clear, and respectful.

They avoid what feels demanding, confusing, or performative.

The pattern repeats everywhere humans decide.

The Quiet Truth, Restated

People do not want to be persuaded.

They want to feel understood.

When they do, decisions stop feeling risky and start feeling resolved.

That's not manipulation.

That's alignment.

The Sale That Already Happened

If you've ever looked back at a decision and realized you made it long before you could explain it, you already understand this book.

All this did was give language to something you've felt for years.

The sale you're trying to make may already be over.

The only question left is whether you'll disrupt it or let it be.

A Final Graybeard Note

Say less.

Design more.

Listen longer.

If you do, you'll discover something quietly liberating:

You won't need to sell as much anymore.

People will arrive already decided.

And you'll both pretend that's not what just happened.

Other Timeless Books in the Graybeard Lectures Series:

Each stands alone.
Together, they form a unique, common sense curriculum.

Graybeard Lectures: Marketing

Drawn from smudged whiteboards and lived experience, This book cuts through buzzwords and trends to reveal how branding, storytelling, word of mouth, and purpose actually work—by understanding humans first. Warm, humorous, and practical, it's a guide for anyone who wants marketing that makes sense and lasts.

Graybeard Lectures: Advertising

Advertising doesn't fail because people stopped paying attention. It fails because it forgets how attention works.

This book explores why the most effective advertising aligns with human instincts rather than fighting them. It examines timing, context, repetition, and emotional truth without chasing trends or tactics.

Graybeard Lectures: Market Research

Listening Past The Numbers is a clear-eyed look at why market research often delivers confidence instead of understanding. It challenges the misuse of data, dashboards, and statistics, arguing for research grounded in human behavior, context, and judgment. Rather than offering tools, the book offers a wiser way to think, listen, and decide when the numbers start acting certain.

Graybeard Lectures: Branding

Branding is not decoration. It's definition.

This book challenges the modern habit of treating brands as visual projects instead of behavioral ones. Logos matter less than promises kept. Consistency matters more than cleverness. Reputation is built slowly and lost quickly.

About the Author

Mark "*Dr. Maddog*" Donnelly, PhD, is the graybeard lecturer who turned a squeaky whiteboard and a tie-dye shirt into a teaching philosophy. A marketing professor, brand consultant, author of 50+ books, historian, photographer, and creative instigator, he's spent decades making complex ideas feel simple – and making students wonder if it's all that coffee he drinks-, or is he naturally this intense.

Dr. Donnelly built his reputation the old-fashioned way: by simplifying the truth. Not the buzzword-stuffed, corporate-approved version, but the real, human kind you only learn after watching trends rise, fall, and come back wearing different shoes.

Along with over 30 years of academia, he's wandered through newspapers, publishing, consulting, community work, and philanthropic strategy – collecting stories, experience, and more old books than any one man needs. Today, his whiteboard scribbles still inspire everyone from Master classes to CEOs, finally captured in print before the janitor could erase them.

Ask him what he truly is and he'll shrug:

> "A teacher at heart.
>
> A storyteller by accident.
>
> A graybeard by mileage."

He lives and creates in Buffalo, New York, with his bride Princess Laura and an ever-expanding pile of notebooks and half-finished ideas. His lifelong principle remains simple:

Make a difference.

This book is his latest attempt to do exactly that.

www.ingramcontent.com/pod-product-compliance
Lightning Source LLC
Chambersburg PA
CBHW040141270326
41928CB00022B/3286